J-Honey Introduces:

"A Spoonful of Honey"

J-Honey Introduces:

"A Spoonful of Honey"

Jacqueline J. Crann

iUniverse, Inc.
New York   Bloomington

iUniverse books may be ordered through booksellers or by contacting:

iUniverse
1663 Liberty Drive
Bloomington, IN 47403
www.iuniverse.com
1-800-Authors (1-800-288-4677)

ISBN: 978-1-4401-3319-0 (sc)
ISBN: 978-1-4401-3320-6 (ebook)

Printed in the United States of America

iUniverse rev. date: 03/26/2009

Contents

"You're a princess, and I'm the castle!"
    ~Words from a three-year-old boy to his mother.

Acknowledgements

Thank you to God, my creator, you never cease to amaze me. Thanks to my son MaliQ. This book would not have been possible if it were not for you. To my parents, my siblings and the rest of my family for all your support. I love you very much. To my old and dear friends, I love you too. To my new friends, thanks for coming into my life. Thanks to Derek George for all your hard work in getting this book published. Thanks so much to Kevin Royer for inspiring, and believing in me. Thanks to Teren Ford, Siea Stubberfield, and Kiffeny Drayton for staying up late at night, and listening to what I wrote. To Chanie Gluck who gave me my first real poetry book. Mo Beasley, thank you for your great input. To Kathleen & Tracey O'Connor, Lisa Collins, Fiona Phillips, Sharon Brooks, Shirley Lewis, Billy Jean Betrand, Lena Williams, and Rhonda Wilson for your great advice when I really needed it. Thank you to Glena and Glado Gladstone, I'll never forget your kindness. To the Cooper family for welcoming me into their home. To my son's teachers, and to all my friends at "Little Miss Muffin". To my friend Sean Reece, thank you for believing in me. I also want to acknowledge Carl Gentiles, Rose Pierre, K. Rougier and Jozelyn Davis, as well as all the people I may have forgotten to mention, and to the one who inspired me to write poetry before I even realized I had talent, you know who you are Mr. West.

"A Spoonful of Honey"

What if?

Feeling all alone,
trembling with the thought of the unknown.
"Passengers, please board the plane"
the flight attendant says.
Palms are sweating
as I try to put my luggage
in the storage up above.
It slips out of my hands
almost hitting a passenger sitting in front.
"What if?" keeps going through my mind.
"What if?" as tears are streaming out the corners of my eyes.
"What if?" as I think of my life packed in two suitcases.
"What if?" as I'm standing there all alone;
What if I made the wrong decision, so far away from home?

The Big Apple

It was really dark,
but the bright beaming lights were attractive.
I couldn't believe it,
I was finally here.
New York City,
the place I dreamed about all my life.
The city that was once a movie to me,
just became my reality.

Who am I?

Who am I?
I am the substance of life, the passageway to earth,
that's created in darkness, but manifested in the light.
Who are you?
You have the perseverance to set forth the way,
to go through the tunnel,
lead you to the passage way.
Why are we here?
We are a visual pleasure,
for the world to see.
Divine minds that can build a divine nation.
Who am I?
Life's first reflection,
also made strong enough to give childbirth to a whole nation.
Who are you?
You are like the sun that shines so bright,
power, strength and energy to last the whole day, until night.
What are we doing here?
I'm a woman, you're a man,
to connect together as one,
that was the plan.
Who am I?
I represent a Queen,
Knowledge, Grace, and wisdom.
Can stand on my own throughout life's tough situations.
Who are you?

You are a King without the armour.
A man that stands tall doesn't need a army,
can stand tall on his own.
What are we doing here?
You are the Thunder before the Storm.
I am the rain that follows, that brings growth to all life's forms.
Who am I?
Beauty, but also wise,
a image that God imagined
for a man to see in his sight
Who are you?
You are like a Tree standing tall,
grounded so deep into the earth.
What are we doing here?
We are here because our creator wanted it that way.
Like he created the moon and the stars,
we all have our place. Who am I?
I am what I was created to be!

Mama's Love

All sticky from having syrup on his pancake from breakfast,
"Mama I love you! Can I have a hug and a kiss?"
Muddy and wet from head to toe, from playing outside in the puddles,
"Mama I love you! Can I have a hug and a kiss?"
Sand in his hair and covering the floor, after playing in the sand pit,
"Mama I love you! Can I have a hug and a kiss?
Helping himself to gooey honey and jam which is on his face and hands,
"Mama I love you! Can I have a hug and a kiss?"
Running towards me with juice, spilling down his shirt and pants,
"Mama I love you! Can I have a hug and a kiss?"
After having a fight with the paints, and paint brush, play dough smeared
all over his body,
Even stuck to his toes.
"Mama I love you! Can I have a hug and a kiss?"
Big Brown Eyes, Golden Brown Skin, chocolate all over his chin.
"Mama I love you! Can I have a hug and a kiss?"

The Tree

Did you ever stop and think
what it would be like to be a tree?
Roots so deeply planted into solid earth.
Seeing everything and everyone
walking around you.
Do they ever think?
I wonder if they do?
Like how we think
of who we want to screw!
Do they think about having babies too?
Having one, two, three and four
Planted outside people's doors?
Do they love other trees?
Or admire each other's leaves?
The different shades,
they change in the Fall
Yellows, Browns, Reds, Oranges and all.
Do they get sad when their leaves are not there anymore?
And they see them on the floor.
Do they get excited when it rains?
Do they have hearts that beat fast
when they feel pain?
Do they get judged by the color
of their bark?

Or is it frustrating when their branches
are not hard and they don't stand
tall like they used to anymore?
I do often think
what it would be like to be a tree,
and I'm so happy that I'm me.

Untitled

●

Sun rises, morning follows.
Sun set dawns, evening begins.
Light disappears, night's near.
Rain falls, flowers bloom.
Trees grow, leaves die.
After death comes life.

Perfect

I hear the whisper of your voice,
as soft as a prayer.
The warmth of your breath upon my lips.
I feel the gentle touch of your hands next to mine,
but thou art rough like a rugged rock,
yet as harmless as a white dove.

Unspoken Silence in the Room

There was an unspoken silence as we lay in the dark.
Both had so much to say, but it wouldn't come out.
I wanted to tell him how I feel.
I wanted to ask, is he for real?
But it wasn't the right time.
He wasn't ready for this heart of mine.
So we laid together, holding one another,
with an unspoken silence in the room.

Lonely

I'm feeling lonely.
You just left me in the cold.
I guess I didn't mean anything to you at all.
I thought we had something special.
That was all in my mind.
When I asked what I meant to you,
you couldn't even describe.
As I lay next to you
with tears rolling down my eyes.
I can't help but wonder,
what's really going on with you inside.
I guess I'll never know,
because you are not open
to that topic of conversation.
So for now, I guess I'll lay here and cry
all alone in the dark.

Palpitations

●

My heart is pumping,
Palpitations like never before.
I feel weak,
I drop to the floor.
I think I'm having a cardiac arrest,
I feel like my heart is coming out of my chest.
I have fallen, and I can't get up.
The only thing that can revive me is your touch.
How would you know this?
You're not around.
But if you don't come quick,
this beating heart will start to slow down.
So hurry where ever you are,
Ohh! I hear a siren!
It's not that far!
The ambulance is getting near,
When they open the door,
I see you appear.
How did you know I was dying?
I heard your heart beat.
I felt your tear drops.
I knew you-was crying,
crying out for my touch.
I knew once I got here,
it wouldn't take much,
to get that heart beat on track.

I've always loved you, and that's a sure fact.
Why didn't you say anything before?
Why wait till I fall to the floor?
Why wait until my heart beat is slow?
And I'm not sure that my heart beat
is there any more.

Road Rules

Love is like a traffic light,
One moment everything is green so green, its perfect.
It's like a smooth ride, finest music playing while holding hands,
Baby kisses in between you glancing at one another.
Its like GPS Navigation always wanting to know where you are,
wanting you near and not far.
You think nothing can go wrong,
then suddenly the lights turn yellow.
The ride starts to slow down.
The holding of the hands are not as often as before.
You start to look at others,
when you never did that before.
You notice a few things you don't like.
Do you keep going,
even though you don't like what you see in your sight?
Or do you stop, before you see the red light?
Most of the time we keep going,
till we run the red light.
We may even run it several times,
because we refuse to see the signs.
Or is it that we're color blind?
Or is it the fear of being alone?

Why we follow our own rules
and manual on love.
Don't go the wrong direction.
Get a map if you have to.
Protect your heart from
getting into an accident.
There's already too many broken hearts!

New York City Morning

New York City is awake
with the sounds of the streets.
Children yelling, going to school,
cars and buses beeping their horns.
The cab driver screaming at the guy in front,
"Damn will you hurry up!"
You hear the sound of the drums
by the homeless man at the subway station.
The jingling of change
from the woman who says
she hasn't ate in days,
"Can I have a quarter, nickel, dime?"
as she stands there with her cup
and looks you dead in the eye.
It's hard to say no.
When she cries "I have AIDS you know!"
"Excuse me please! Do you mind?"
says a passenger who just got hit in the side.
"Have a nice day" says the conductor
as you exit the subway.
It's Thursday, only one more day.
And then it's the weekend again.
Hearing sounds of the elevator door.

"Third floor please"
That's my stop.
As I see my boss looking at her clock.
Its five-past nine.
Five minutes late.
I hope she doesn't dock my pay.
"Good morning!" you say
when you answer the phone.
I can't wait till five
when it's time to go home!

Fly

Sometimes I feel so lonely inside.
I feel like a caterpillar who wants to crawl away and hide.
Then come out as a butterfly,
challenge this world, and fly.
Fly to where my destiny leads me to be,
maybe Africa, Europe or even the Islands!
Right now I feel I could fly.
Way up high, almost near the sky!
Like a bird looking for food,
or a bee looking for flowers.
I could even be a helicopter,
flying over houses.
Maybe fly to where there's a whole different environment,
where I can meet people who
speak different languages.
Or fly where you see kids running bare feet.
Or seeing people wearing tribal wear,
for real! not for fun.
Not living in a house,
instead in a hut.
Flying right now is a place I want to be,
until wherever my destiny leads me;
somewhere I can be,
happy, free, and me.

Will we meet again?

As the blue bird flew into the sky.
I wondered where he may fly.
I watched him until he faded away.
"Where did that blue bird fly?" I did say
Will I ever see him again by my way?
Will he ever come for bread
that I spread upon my window ledge?
Will we again meet eye to eye?
Or was that our goodbye?

Summer's Day

Oh how I compare thee to a summer's day.
How the ray of the sun shines down
and glows upon thy lovely face.
How beautiful to see the colorful flowers bloom,
like you smile in the month of June.
Oh what a delight to hear your voice,
it's like the birds singing in the early 'morn.
Oh how wonderful to feel your touch,
as soft as silk and gentle as rain,
when it falls lightly upon one's face.
Oh how outstanding thou art,
you shine like the moon,
and beam like the stars
Oh how I compare thee to a summer's day.

Autumn Day

What a beautiful Autumn Day.
The type of day you want to stay,
and never go away.
Everyone seems to have a smile on their face,
the weather has that effect some days.

Ocean Breeze

The sea is gently roaring.
The ocean breeze is blowing.
It reminds me of that voice,
it's so calming.

Sunrise

My eyes are shining bright,
like two stars in the sky.
From being in your presence,
in the midst of the night.
We sat and held each other
as the music played.
Not wanting the night to end,
as we passionately kissed.
A kiss so soft it absorbed
every part of our bodies.
Nervous laughs we both did
as we glanced at each other.
As we sat there in silence,
until the sunset-rised.

Reflections

I was thinking about you today,
it felt so good.
The way you touch, and caress me,
hands so tender, the way you kiss,
your warm soft lips pressing against mine,
the way you look at me after we've kissed.
I'm in such bliss.
I love how you rub my thighs.
As you look me in the eyes.
I sigh, because it feels so nice.
As we lay there together in the moment.
It just feels right.
Our bodies connect so tight.
As we embrace face to face,
drifting off to a special place.
Chills running down my spine,
just by your touch,
imagining that you are mine.
I love being around you.
Your energy and presence
makes me feel at a comfortable place.
Peaceful and pleasant.

Our surroundings are like the cool ocean breeze
Golden brown sand and palm trees
Sun shining so bright,
we can see our reflection in the clear blue sea.
I can see you, can you see me?
Look at us, we were meant to be.

Walk sweetly in Life

I have you on my mind all the time.
It makes me happy when I think of your smile.
Your smile is like a ray of sunshine
that shines down on the earth to give light.
Your energy is so amazing,
it's like a like a volt of electricity
that gives off power to every room.
This is what happens when you walk into a room.
You stand out from the rest.
You are definitely in a league by yourself.
When God was thinking about creating man,
he had you for his plan.
I've seen flowers in Spring Time Grow,
and the sounds of the Oceans roar,
But I've never met anyone, quite like you before.

The Feelings I have inside!

What is this I am feeling inside?
Love, love I can not hide?
What do I do? How do I control this?
Do I ignore these feelings I have inside?
Or put my heart right in your hands?
Would this be wise at this time?
Letting you know how I am feeling inside?
You may break this sensitive heart of mine.
If you are tuned into me then you'll know.
My eyes say it all.
These eyes of mine cannot hide
these feelings I have inside.
Do you feel the way I do?
I guess the only way to know is to tell you.
Let you know what's on my mind
These feelings are eating me alive inside.
Why are they bursting to come out so?
They're crying out loud, let the world know how much I love you so
It's scary, but it's true.
The only way to know is to tell you about these feelings of mine,
but please don't break this sensitive heart of mine.

The Feelings I have Inside [Part II]

I'm wondering what's going on in your mind.
How you feel about me?
Or will you break this sensitive heart of mine?
Do you like what you see?
Not on the outside, but within.
You always say I am beautiful,
but what is beauty to you?

Twisted Woman

You've got me twisted!
Body bent-up.
Thinking about you.
You have me crossing my legs,
standing on my head.
Crazy for you.
You have me touching my toes,
doing splits to the floor.
Head over heels for you.
You have me doing hand-stands,
Crawling down the wall.
Walking like a crab.
Infatuated by you.
You have me doing Yoga, Ty-Bo and Jujitsu.
Having my body going crazy for you.
You have me dancing to the floor, till I can't dance no-more.
Head over heels for you.
You've got me doubled up in pain, crying and shouting your name.
Twisted, and in love with you!

Twisted Man

●

You've got me hiding in my car,
waiting 'til you come home at night!
Fighting with your cousin,
thinking you've got another man.
You've got me losing sleep at night.
Thinking of your pretty face,
I can't even eat!
You've got me in a daze.
You've got me walking down the street,
just thinking of you.
Not knowing what the F_ _ K I am gonna do.
You've got me saying your name over and over again.
I don't know what you did to me,
but your love is driving me insane.
You've got me cancelling with my boys so I can be with you.
My boys are telling me,
that I am Twisted and in love with you.
You've got me going to the Gym pumping crazy weights,
trying to get my body tight,
so that you don't go any place.
You've got me thinking about having a family,
having marriage on my mind.

I never even thought of marriage
until you came into my life.
Tell me what I need to do
to make you 100% mine.
Your love has got me twisted,
I want to make you my wife.

Love, Love, Love

I want real love.
Love you can not hide.
When you meet that special one,
they make you all tingly inside.
Have you knocked off your feet,
have you begging for their love constantly.
Has you wanting it more and more,
like a kid wanting candy, from a candy store.
You want to overflow
So you never run out.
Like you do when you go shopping
at Cosco's Discount.
Has you shouting out loud,
saying thank you lord,
not for a good night of sex.
But for that companion of yours.
Has you thinking at work,
"When is it five?"
Just can't wait
to look into your loved one's eyes.
You don't have to do anything,
just be around each other.
chilling, eating popcorn
while watching your favorite movie,
" Love Jones".

Holding hands, as Darius reads Nina love poems.
Just feeling their vibe because you know how they feel.
Their love is for real.
Love that goes right to the core.
You just want to bottle-it-up and sell it in the stores.
Love so real you want the whole world to know.
When you find this kind of love,
you don't need to look no-more.
God gave you the perfect one
Who completes you,
like Claire did Cliff on the Cosby Show.
This is what I want, no doubt.
I won't settle for less.
I want real love in my life.
It's the Best!

Colour of love

The love we share is beautiful to see.
It's like a picture on a canvas
that fits a room so perfectly.

Shopping with you!

I imagine you in the store trying on some clothes,
waiting behind the fitting room door.
Taking a peek every 10 seconds,
looking at that tight sexy body of yours.
Dark, smooth, cut in all the right places.
As you stand there looking tall,
and so dammmn fine! finer than wine.
The fragrance of sandalwood
wafting from your well-groomed locks.
I asked "can I join you?" "sure!" you reply.
As I step inside, you stand behind me.
You position yourself in between my golden brown thighs,
Uhhhhhhh Arrrrrrrrrrrrr it feels so nice!
I close my eyes enjoying the moment.
We hear a knock on the door, "is everything alright?"
We say "fine!" as our bodies are entwined.
Not wanting to let go of each other as the feeling was so right.
As we both explode together with a feeling of ecstasy!
We walk out the fitting room door with a smile you couldn't ignore.
When the assistant asked do you want any of the clothes?
We both sigh, "ahhhhhhhhhhhhhhhh!"
"No thanks miss, the fit was Tight!"

Lust at First Sight!

He saw me, watching him, checking me out,
while waiting for the elevator to arrive.
He glanced at my pretty toes.
As we walked through the elevator door,
our eyes made four.
He was standing behind me,
I felt his warm breath at the back of my neck.
He leaned over me to press his floor.
I couldn't ignore his lips.
He had the kind that leaves you with such bliss.
The type that makes you think out loud.
"Oooohhh!!!!!" I couldn't help it, just came out.
I was feeling aroused!
My nipples were hard like I was cold,
but I was hot like a steam kettle on a hot stove.
I started sweating in between my thighs,
I'm about to have a orgasm,
I hope he doesn't realize.
You could see it in my eyes that I was mesmerized.
This man was fine.
I almost missed my floor, he had me in a trance.
As I'm walking out the elevator he holds the door,
"Hey Miss, I'm sorry but what's your name?"
"Honey..." my little voice says,
As the elevator door closes!

Lust at First Sight [Part II]

🌢

Why didn't I tell him
he caught my eye?
Why didn't I tell him
he had the sexiest voice
I've heard in a long time?
Why didn't I tell him
I was lusting to taste
those gorgeous lips of his?
Why didn't I tell him,
I was sweating by the air
of his breath at the back of my neck?
Why didn't I tell him
He had such energy
like the Matrix Part I, II and III?
Why didn't I say something
When I saw him glance at my toes?
When our eyes made four?
Now it's too late
The elevator door is closed!

Who is he?

Who is he?
Is he the one I saw in my dream?
Dark like a berry that you picked off the tree.
As I walk into the room, he's the first thing my eyes see.
I'm not wearing my contacts, but my vision is clear,
like I would see in my dream!
Who is he?
Is he the one I saw in my dream?
His eyes are my favorite shade of brown, they see right through me.
Like I just ate the apple in the garden of E.
Who is he?
Is he the one I saw in my dream?
He talks to me without opening his mouth, it's so comforting.
His presence with mine, is like the sunshine without the clouds
Who is he?
Is he the one I saw in my dream?
I didn't know when you was coming,
but I knew you before you even seen me.
Who am I?
Open your eyes!
You've been looking for me since the beginning of time.
That's why we met, you just don't know it yet.
I'm the one you saw in your dream!

Playing on my mind

I thought I saw you today.
He looked just like you.
The way you walk, how you dress.
He even smiled at me the way you do.
But it wasn't you,
it was someone else.
I thought I saw you today.
I even said your name.
I tapped you on the shoulder,
when I saw that confused look on his face.
But it wasn't you,
it was someone else.
I thought I saw you today.
I said it's been a long time,
nice to see you again.
Then I realized,
it wasn't you.
It was someone else.
I really wish I could see you again.
Just one more chance
to feel, to touch,
and to be in your presence,
once again.

Honey's Love

Ten passionate kisses on my forehead,
followed by a full body massage.
Suck on my toes.
That's one way to get me hot.
Whisper sweet things
as are bodies are entwined.
Say something spicy, I definitely won't mind!
Put your tender hand in my long locks,
and the other caress my breasts,
let them touch your face
while are bodies are embraced.
Whip cream is good too,
you can squirt it on my back.
Use that tongue of yours to wipe me up,
like I just took a bubble bath.
Rub me down with sweet oils
as I'm laying so relaxed,
till I finally go to sleep,
with the gentleness of your hands.

Organic Man

He's organic of the best kind,
The type you have to dig deep to find.
Like pushing all the other fruits aside,
because you see that crisp bright seed in sight.
He's the type you don't often see around.
He's organic in every form,
from the way he stands out.
Eve would have stole him from the tree without doubt.
He's organic, deeply rooted,
made so fine.
Organic man, you're one of a kind.

Vegetarian

Strictly veggie, that's me!
Well, I thought I was,
then I saw that tasty piece of meat!
A slice that looked so lean,
dark, and well-done;
looking so attractive and neat!

Patiently

●

Why are we so afraid of our own inner being?
Is it because we don't trust our own inner feelings?
I stand there like a flower so tall.
Waiting for the right bee to come.
A bee that has just the right sting,
realizes the quality of honey he's wanting.
Recognizes exactly which flower is his type.
Doesn't buzz around being confused by his sight.
Knows where he's going to fall.
His flower is deeply rooted and all.
May take him a little longer to get to the root,
but he knows the Quality of Pollen that he suits.

Touch

These hands, they are gentle,
but at the same time very strong.
Can make your whole body go weak,
with one simple touch.
A woman's hands.

Hearts

In life I've met so many different hearts.
Hearts in love, happy hearts, lonely hearts.
Hearts so big you could fit this whole world in it.
Kind Hearts, mean hearts, weak hearts, sick hearts,
crying out for attention hearts.
Hearts that have you wondering if there is a heart.
But the most memorable heart of all,
would have to be the broken heart.
Once in love so deep,
and did not see the storm coming in their direction.
So be careful with your heart.
Treasure it.
Once broken, could take a lifetime to mend.

The Bee came out in Spring

Buzzing-Bee, what do you want from me?
My beautiful bright petals?
My long slender stem?
My sweet fragrance of nature?
A little taste of my pure honey?
Buzzing bee, what do you want from me?
Out of all the flowers in the garden,
Why did you pick me?
Is it the way I'm deeply-rooted,
or well-maintained?
I'm not sure what it is,
but your buzzing is driving me insane.
I don't feel like being bothered
on this warm spring day.
Please, please Mr. Bee,
will you go away!

Unforgettable

Ten tiny fingers,
Ten little toes,
eyes that look so peaceful,
and a small button nose.
A heart-beat racing,
A teardrop in the eye
As the doctor says, "He's perfect"
A mother's first sonogram.

Connect

When we walk into the room,
are they looking at me?
or looking at you?
We have this kind of chemistry,
that everyone can surely see.
It has people staring all the time.
It's a chemistry they want to find.
As they look at how we react.
How they wish they could have that.
It's a connection that is so unique.
You knock me off my feet.
I love the way you make me feel.
It's a friendship that is so real.

What you see.

You see the sky so blue,
and the moon and stars shine so bright.
The color of the leaves that turn every season.
You see the ocean waves,
and the golden brown sands.
The bright yellow sun that shines up above.
You see flowers of all types.
Red, yellow, pink, green, purple, orange and blue
You see the power of the rain after a storm,
when you see a rainbow form.
You see happy, sad and anger after pain,
that sometimes doesn't go away.
You see men, women, children of all types,
different, but formed to be on this earth.
You see Africa memories bright
Children, homes, the land and all the surroundings.
You see disappointment, dishonesty, lies, deceit.
You see sex, lust, hearts, love.
All these things you see,
but do you see me?

Moving

●

I am sitting here on the bus,
looking at everyone going by.
It's cold outside, the wind is blowing.
People's bodies are moving side-to-side.
The force of the breeze
is blowing the trees.
The sky is so blue,
with only a few clouds way up high
It looks beautiful,
even though the forecast says snow.
Maybe it will, or maybe it won't.
Only god knows what this weather will bring.
But I do know,
it's a beautiful day for sure.

Garden.

In the garden there are flowers,
all different kinds.
All pretty colors, looking so bright.
But there is one special flower
that has this certain glow.
That could only be you;
You know.

Love Yourself

I love me.
Every part of me.
From head to toe.
I just want the world to know,
It feels so good
loving me.
I walk with my head high,
a confidence that everyone can see
I love my big almond-shaped eyes
My full lips, my teeth
the way I smile.
My long nose,
my thick locks,
my slender shape,
all the things about me that God made,
So when you look in the mirror,
love what you see,
God made you special,
just like he made me.